Yoga Sutras

The Sayings of Patanjali

A New English Version

Bart Marshall

REALFACE PRESS

Introduction

The *Yoga Sutras of Patanjali* were written around the time of Jesus, give or take 200 years. The practice of yoga began in India as early as 1000 years prior, but the *Yoga Sutras* are the most important compendium of this ancient oral tradition, and virtually all later schools of yoga begin with Patanjali.

Little is known about him, but there is evidence he was an educated philosopher, grammarian, and physician—a long-lost medical work is attributed to him. No doubt he received oral instruction in yoga and probably lived in remote caves, forests, and river banks, which were the most frequent practicing grounds of the time. At some point, enlightenment happened.

Why he committed an oral tradition to written text is unknown, but as the remote meditative havens of the yogis receded and dedicated aspirants dwindled, he may have feared that yoga would become forgotten, lost, or corrupted. Regardless, we are the beneficiaries of his efforts.

The literal meaning of the word *sutra* is "thread," which by extension and usage has come to connote "spiritual instruction." Simple, direct, practical—yet not easily understood or practiced—the threads of Patanjali weave an elegant system for opening the door to Self-realization.

1. Unity

1.1
OM. What follows are instructions on Unity.

1.2
Unity obtains when the activities of mind have ceased.

1.3
The witness then abides in its true nature.

1.4
Otherwise, the witness is identified with the activities of mind and is just another thought-form itself.

1.5
There are five types of mind activity, both painful and pleasurable.

1.6
These are: correct perception, misperception, imagination, dreamless sleep, and memory.

1.7
Correct perception may derive from direct observation, valid reasoning or accurate testimony of enlightened teachers.

1.8
Misperception is knowledge based on the illusion of forms, rather than on the true nature of reality.

1.9
Imagination is mental images derived from words and concepts rather than objective observation and sensory perceptions.

1.10
Dreamless sleep is the state of mind when thought is absent and sensory perception is in abeyance.

1.11
Memory is the retention of thoughts and images generated by sensory perception and imagination.

1.12
Cessation of mind activity is achieved through the practice of *yoga* and the habit of dispassionate non-attachment.

1.13
Yoga practice is the willful effort to restrain the five activities of mind and abide in a state of stillness.

1.14
To be firmly grounded, this practice must be performed with earnestness

and devotion over a long period of time,
all the while holding the goal in clear
and constant view.

1.15
Dispassionate non-attachment
is the absence of desire for experiences
of the senses — seen and unseen,
here and hereafter.

1.16
Supreme dispassion is indifference
to the three *gunas* of creation —
light, inertia and vibration —
owing to a direct knowledge of Self.

1.17
Meditation for direct-knowing of the
objective world is fourfold in nature:
exterior observation, inner perception,
alert stillness, and the sense "I Am."

1.18
The other state of meditation is when awareness perceives no thought or object—only the seeds of unmanifested possibilities.

1.19
It is the natural state of formless beings and those absorbed in True Nature.

1.20
Others can attain it through faith, earnestness, self-inquiry, clarity, and insight.

1.21
Those who proceed with unshakable intent can attain this state quickly.

1.22
Those who practice with varying degrees of effort—mild, moderate, intense—will succeed in accordance with their efforts.

1.23
The other way to attain the natural state is through surrender to God.

1.24
God is the Supreme Being, formless, unbounded, limitless, untouched by action and desire.

1.25
The omniscience of God is infinite. Man has but a germ of awareness.

1.26
God is timeless, the ever-present Master of the ancient masters.

1.27
He is called by OM.

1.28
Silently repeat this word as a mantra while meditating upon its significance.

1.29
From this comes the disappearance
of obstacles to the realization of Self.

1.30
The obstacles to Self-realization are
disease, inertia, doubt, carelessness,
procrastination, laziness, sense cravings,
false perception, inability to concentrate,
and inability to stabilize higher states
when attained.

1.31
Encountering these obstacles
one experiences grief, despair,
physical agitation, and anxious breathing.

1.32
To overcome these obstacles, the constant
practice of a single truth is required.

1.33
The mind can be stilled by the earnest practice of openness, compassion, virtue, and indifference.

1.34
Or by breathing in and out, intentionally.

1.35
Intentional focus on any sense experience will enhance perception and still the mind.

1.36
Concentration upon the inner light beyond sorrow stills the mind.

1.37
Meditation upon a transcendent being stills the mind.

1.38
Inquiring into the experiences of dreams and dreamless sleep stills the mind.

1.39
Fixing attention on that which is nearest the heart, also stills the mind.

1.40
The stilled mind of a *yoga* master realizes everything, from the infinitely small to the infinitely great.

1.41
As pure crystal takes on the adjacent colors, so does the mind free of thought become indistinguishable from that which it contemplates. The perceiver, the act of perceiving, and the object perceived are seen as one.

1.42
When the mind projects names
and concepts on what is seen
through direct perception,
confusion and delusion result.

1.43
When the mind is clear,
empty of memories and knowledge,
things are seen exactly as they are.

1.44
These same two conditions – projection
and clarity – also apply to the perception
of subtle, unmanifest realms.

1.45
The observation of progressively more
subtle realms leads to the primal source.

1.46
All these meditations have separate
perceptions as their seed.

1.47
When there is no perception of separateness, the supreme Self reigns.

1.48
And absolute Truth is revealed as self-evident.

1.49
The direct experience of Truth is nothing like intellectual knowledge gained from scriptures and teachings.

1.50
The direct experience of Truth supercedes and destroys all previous impressions.

1.51
When the impression of a direct experience of Truth is also wiped out, there remains only awareness without seed.

2. Practice

2.1
Purification, self-inquiry,
and surrender to God
are the practices that lead to Unity.

2.2
These practices cultivate awareness
and remove the afflictions that obstruct
realization of Truth.

2.3
The obstructing afflictions are ignorance,
false sense of self, desire, aversion,
and a tenacious clinging to life.

2.4
Ignorance is the origin of all other
afflictions—the pre-emergent and
the vestigial, the nearly-overcome
and the fully operational.

2.5

Ignorance regards the impermanent as permanent, the impure as pure, the bad as good, the ego self as true Self.

2.6

The false ego self is born when the instrument of seeing is mis-identified as being separate from the One who sees.

2.7

Desire is attachment to pleasure.

2.8

Aversion is attachment to the absence of suffering.

2.9

Tenacious clinging to life is inherent in all beings, from the most ignorant to the most wise. Life after life, it is sustained by its own momentum.

2.10
When these five afflictions have become subtle, vestigial, they can be destroyed by abiding in their opposites.

2.11
When they are fully operational, they must be overcome through meditation.

2.12
Mental and physical actions rooted in these afflictions bear fruit as experiences in this and future lifetimes.

2.13
For so long as the roots exist, they bear fruit as fortune of birth, length of life, and the experience of pleasure or suffering.

2.14
The pleasure or suffering you experience is the fruit of your good or bad actions.

2.15
One who is spiritually aware sees that all experience is suffering, due to constant change, anxiety, forces of nature, and imprints of subliminal processes.

2.16
Suffering yet to come can be avoided.

2.17
Suffering is caused by the illusion that there is an experiencer to whom an experience is happening.

2.18
Everything perceived is composed of the three *gunas* of creation—light, inertia, and vibration. These form the elements as well as the senses, which interact to create experience and the path to liberation from it.

2.19
The three *gunas* flow in four states – gross, subtle, primal, and unmanifest.

2.20
The witness is Self – pure awareness – which, though boundless and unchanging, appears to perceive creation through the construct of mind.

2.21
The existence of all that is, serves Self-awareness alone.

2.22
One who attains Unity sees creation is not real, yet creation persists because it is taken by others as real.

2.23
The identification of pure awareness with the mind and the creations of the mind

causes the apprehension of both an objective world and a perceiver of it.

2.24
This identification is ignorance. It must be overcome.

2.25
When this identification is broken, ignorance vanishes, liberation is attained, and Self realizes its true nature.

2.26
Liberation is attained through unwavering intent and discernment.

2.27
The way of Self-realization progresses through seven stages.

2.28
Steady practice of the means of *yoga* dissolves impurities and invites illumination of the Real.

2.29
The eight means of *yoga* are self-restraint, faithful observance, right posture, intentional breathing, sense withdrawal, concentration, meditation,
and awareness.

2.30
The five pillars of self-restraint are non-violence, truthfulness, honesty, celibacy, and non-attachment.

2.31
These great practices are valid for all — irrespective of social class, location, time or circumstance — and thus constitute the universal Way.

2.32
The five observances are purification, contentment, aspiration, study, and surrender to God.

2.33
To be free of thoughts contrary to *yoga*, opposite thoughts must be cultivated.

2.34
Contrary thoughts leading to acts of violence, dishonesty, and lust—whether personally done, caused to be done, or merely approved of—arise from greed, anger and ignorance, and whether mild, moderate or intense, they perpetuate suffering and delusion. This is why their opposites must be cultivated.

2.35
In the presence of one who is grounded in non-violence, enmity is not possible.

2.36
When one is obedient to Truth, what he says and does becomes what is true.

2.37
When one is established in non-stealing, wealth flows to him.

2.38
One who is steadfast in celibacy acquires spiritual energy, strength, and courage.

2.39
One who is unattached and free
of cravings, gains insight into all of life –
past, present, and yet to come.

2.40
Physical and mental purification
produces an indifference to one's own
body, and ends one's infatuation
with the bodies of others.

2.41
One who is pure of heart obtains serenity of spirit, power of concentration, control of the senses, and the capacity to directly realize Self.

2.42
Through contentment one attains bliss.

2.43
The fire of aspiration burns through impurities and heightens the powers of the body and senses.

2.44
Through self inquiry and spiritual study one attains communion
with the object of study.

2.45
Through surrender to God one realizes clear Awareness.

2.46
Right posture is to be seated in a manner both solid and relaxed.

2.47
Effortless stillness is achieved by focusing the mind on the boundless realm.

2.48
Here, the opposites hold no sway.

2.49
When right posture is attained,
the practice of intentional breathing
then follows.

2.50
Intentional breathing controls the three phases of breath—exhalation, inhalation, and hiatus. Breathing can be regulated by controlling the spacing, depth, number, and duration of breaths.

2.51
There is a fourth level of breath so subtle it transcends the realm of internal and external sense objects.

2.52
Through these practices the veil that obscures the inner light is lifted.

2.53
And the mind becomes capable of concentrating attention.

2.54
When the mind withdraws attention from sense experience, the senses receive no impressions from sense objects, and awareness rests in its essential nature.

2.55
In this way, complete mastery of the senses is achieved.

3. Powers

3.1
Concentration is the unwavering focus of attention on a single object in consciousness.

3.2
Meditation is the effortless flow of sustained concentration.

3.3
Reflection is when objects in consciousness are experienced directly, free of mind, with no degree of separation.

3.4
Concentration, meditation, reflection. These three constitute *samyama* — detached awareness.

3.5
Through mastery of *samyama*,
the essence of wisdom is illuminated.

3.6
It is applied in stages.

3.7
The three aspects of *samyama* are more intimate and internal than are the five self-restraints previously described.

3.8
But even these are external to the seedless absorption of *samadhi*.

3.9
Thoughts arise from no-thought,
play out, then vanish. In the emptiness
between thoughts, the mind is capable
of self-reflection.

3.10
When thought is absent, the flow of mind is stilled.

3.11
When mental distractions disappear, what remains is one-pointed awareness.

3.12
One-pointedness is when the arising thought and the vanishing thought are the same—with no gap between.

3.13
In this state, the mind passes beyond the realm of forms and sense organs—beyond observation of attributes, ideas of purpose, and perception of apparent change.

3.14
The three properties of specific forms are: potential characteristics, manifest

characteristics, and the unmanifest source common to all forms.

3.15
The interplay of these three properties
creates the appearance
of evolutionary change.

3.16
The practice of *samyama* on the triple-nature of specific forms leads to an understanding of past and future manifestations.

3.17
The sound of a word, the object
it denotes, and the thought conjured up by the word, are confused by the ordinary mind as being the same.
By practicing *samyama* on the distinction between these, the *yogi* comes to understand the meaning of sounds made by all living things.

3.18

By practicing *samyama* on the flow of thought-images, knowledge of previous existence arises.

3.19

By practicing *samyama* on others, knowledge of their thoughts arises.

3.20

However, the object of another's thoughts—being distinct from the thought itself—cannot be known by the practice of *samyama*.

3.21

By practicing *samyama* on the essential nature of his own form, the *yogi* gains control over the emanations that make his body visible to others.

3.22
In this way also, he gains control
of the emanations of sound, smell,
and substance of his body,
and can thus vanish completely
from the senses of others.

3.23
Some actions in life bear fruit quickly.
Others ripen late. By practicing *samyama*
on the *karma* of his life, a *yogi* comes to
know the exact time it will end. This can
also be known through signs and omens.

3.24
By practicing *samyama* on empathy,
compassion, and non-attachment,
one gains union with others.

3.25
By practicing *samyama* on any attribute of an element or animal—such as the strength of an elephant—that attribute will be attained.

3.26
By practicing *samyama* on the inner light, one perceives the subtle, the hidden, the mysterious and minute.

3.27
By practicing *samyama* on the sun, one gains knowledge of the planetary worlds.

3.28
By practicing *samyama* on the moon, one gains knowledge of the positions of stars.

3.29
By practicing *samyama* on the pole star, one gains knowledge of the movement of stars.

3.30
By practicing *samyama* on the center point of the body, one gains knowledge of the systems of the body.

3.31
By practicing *samyama* on the throat center, one gains control over thoughts of hunger and thirst.

3.32
By practicing *samyama* on the "tortoise" nerve duct in the chest, one becomes immovable.

3.33
By practicing *samyama* on the radiant center of the head, one attains vision of perfected beings.

3.34
Also, all these things can be known without *samyama*—in the spontaneous clear light of Realization.

3.35
By practicing *samyama* on the heart,
the workings of one's mind—
and the minds of others—can be known.

3.36
The bondage of experience results from a failure to discriminate between the highest aspects of personal identity and the true Self—which are completely different. The spiritual aspect of personal identity is merely an agent of Self—which is totally independent and exists for its own sake. Practicing *samyama* on personal identity as separate from Self leads to Self-knowledge.

3.37
Through this *samyama* there arises a spontaneous realization, and the powers of hearing, touch, vision, taste, and smell reach beyond the sense organs to the realm of extra-sensory intuition.

3.38
They are powers in worldly experience, but obstacles to *samadhi*.

3.39
When the bonds of sense experience are loosened and the mode of transference understood, the consciousness of a *yogi* can enter another body.

3.40
By mastering the vital force that governs the upper chest, the *yogi* can rise above water, swamps, thorny paths and the like, and ascend at will.

3.41
By mastering the vital force that moves the abdomen, the *yogi* can emit a blazing radiance.

3.42
Through *samyama* on the relationship of the ear to the void comes divine hearing.

3.43
Through *samyama* on the relationship
of the body to the void
comes the lightness of cotton,
and the ability to move through space.

3.44
Through *samyama* on awareness without a body—the Great Incorporeal Awareness—the veil that obscures the light dissolves.

3.45
Through *samyama* on the five aspects of forms – gross manifestation, elemental nature, subtle characteristics, interplay of the three *gunas*, and significance to the observer – the *yogi* obtains mastery over forms.

3.46
Thus he can become the microcosm and attain all other powers, as well as perfect the body – which is no longer subject to laws of form.

3.47
Perfection of the body includes beauty, grace, strength, and the crystal hardness of a diamond.

3.48
Mastery of the senses comes through *samyama* on the mechanism of perception, on the essential nature of the sense

organs, on the sense of personal identity, on the interplay of the three *gunas*, and on the experience being created.

3.49
Thus the *yogi* can move at the speed of thought, perceive without senses, and transmute matter from one form to another.

3.50
Through *samyama* on the distinction between the spiritual component of personal identity and the true Self, one becomes all-knowing and attains mastery over all things.

3.51
Through indifference to all these powers, the seeds of bondage and sorrow are destroyed and Unity is attained.

3.52
When divine beings appear to flatter and invite the *yogi* to join them, attachment and pride must be avoided, otherwise he will fall once more into ignorance.

3.53
Through *samyama* on the smallest moment of time and on the succession of moments, one attains the capacity of discernment.

3.54
Thus one can distinguish between identical objects that cannot be distinguished by species, characteristics, or position in space.

3.55
Wisdom born of discernment delivers one from ignorance. It comprehends all things at once—what has been and will be—in an eternal moment without succession.

3.56
When the mind is as immaculate and clear as Self, liberation occurs and Unity obtains.

4. Liberation

4.1
Spiritual powers can be obtained by birth, or through drugs, incantations, austerities, or meditation.

4.2
The transformation of one form or level of existence to another is the nature of the creative force.

4.3
Deeds and practices are not the direct cause of transformation, but they can clear away obstacles, just as the irrigator clears earth from the watercourse so that water may flow according to its nature.

4.4
It is the sense "I Am" that produces the many minds.

4.5
Though the activities of the many minds are varied, the one original mind controls all.

4.6
Of the many minds, only the mind purified by meditation is freed from experiencing latent *karma*.

4.7
The *karma* of the *yogi* is neither white nor black. The *karma* of others is white, black, or both.

4.8
Of the tendencies inherent in one's *karma*, only those for which environmental conditions are favorable will manifest and ripen.

4.9
Because the imprint of unmanifested tendencies transcends birth and death, the chain of cause and effect is unbroken by changes in form, time, and place.

4.10
Because the desire to exist is eternal, the succession of identity images produced by these tendencies is without beginning.

4.11
These tendencies and identity images are held together by cause and effect, grounded in desire, and stimulated by sense experience. When all these factors are removed, the succession of identity images comes to an end.

4.12
The form and expression called "past" and the form and expression called

"future" exist in the eternal now of objects as properties of their essential nature.

4.13
These properties are either manifest, subtle, or latent according to the interplay of the three *gunas*.

4.14
Because the three *gunas* comprise every form and expression of objects, in reality there is only Unity.

4.15
Though the essential nature of an object is always the same, its material existence is perceived differently by individual minds according to the observer's state of being.

4.16
And so, if an object perceived only by a single mind is no longer cognized by that mind, does it have material existence?

4.17
An object is known or unknown depending on whether or not it is reflected in the mind.

4.18
The Self, lord of the mind,
is the immutable, unchanging witness
of the mind's fluctuations.

4.19
The mind is not self-knowing
since it can be observed as an object.

4.20
Neither can the mind be both
the perceiver and the perceived
simultaneously.

4.21
To postulate an anterior mind perceiving the first, one would have to postulate an infinite series of minds, each perceiving

the one before it, thus causing an endless confusion of percepts and memories.

4.22
The Self is immaculate, unchangeable.
When Self is reflected in the mind,
the mind abides in Self-awareness.

4.23
Self-awareness, reflecting both the knower and the knowable, is omniscient.

4.24
Though the mind has numerous identity imprints and desires, it is merely an agent of Self and cannot act independently for its own sake.

4.25
One who clearly sees this distinction,
no longer confuses the mind with Self.

4.26
The mind then bends to discriminating awareness and is borne onwards to liberation.

4.27
But until liberation, distractions due to imprints and habitual thinking may still arise when discrimination wavers.

4.28
These distractions are similar to the obstacles to Self-realization already mentioned, and can be overcome in the same way.

4.29
One who remains undistracted even by attainment of the highest illumination becomes, as a result of this perfect discrimination, what is called the "Cloud of Virtue."

4.30
Thus comes the end of illusion and freedom from *karma.*

4.31
Then all obstructions and impurities vanish, and in the presence of infinite Knowing, the whole of the sensory universe appears as nothing.

4.32
The interplay of the three *gunas*—light, inertia, vibration—then ceases, having fulfilled their transformative purpose.

4.33
The sequence of changing moments in time begins and ends in the eternal now.

4.34
When the three *gunas* are devoid
of purpose liberation is complete,
Self is revealed as Unity,
and nothing remains to be done.

www.ingramcontent.com/pod-product-compliance
Lightning Source LLC
Chambersburg PA
CBHW040113150726
48005CB00013B/1690

* 9 7 9 8 8 6 8 9 7 3 5 3 6 *